P9-CKZ-991

Wisdom for GRADUATES

© 2010 by Barbour Publishing, Inc.

Compiled by Donna K. Maltese.

ISBN 978-1-60260-713-2

All rights reserved. No part of this publication may be reproduced or transmitted for commercial purposes, except for brief quotations in printed reviews, without written permission of the publisher.

Scripture quotations marked MSG are from ***THE MESSAGE.*** Copyright © by Eugene H. Peterson 1993, 1994, 1995, 1996, 2000, 2001, 2002. Used by permission of NavPress Publishing Group.

Scripture quotations marked NLT are taken from the Holy Bible, New Living Translation, copyright © 1996, 2004. Used by permission of Tyndale House Publishers, Inc. Wheaton, Illinois 60189, U.S.A. All rights reserved.

Scripture quotations marked NKJV are taken from the New King James Version®. Copyright © 1982 by Thomas Nelson, Inc. Used by permission. All rights reserved.

Scripture quotations marked KJV are taken from the King James Version of the Bible.

Scripture quotations marked NIV are taken from the HOLY BIBLE, NEW INTERNATIONAL VERSION®. NIV®. Copyright © 1973, 1978, 1984 by International Bible Society. Used by permission of Zondervan. All rights reserved.

Scripture quotations marked NASB are taken from the New American Standard Bible, © 1960, 1962, 1963, 1968, 1971, 1972, 1973, 1975, 1977, 1995 by The Lockman Foundation. Used by permission.

Published by Barbour Publishing, Inc., P.O. Box 719, Uhrichsville, Ohio 44683, www.barbourbooks.com

Our mission is to publish and distribute inspirational products offering exceptional value and biblical encouragement to the masses.

Printed in India.

Wisdom for GRADUATES

DAY 1

Designing Your Future

What you will become is a matter of conjecture—the great lathe of circumstance is waiting to carve your career. . . . Take time—consider. You are the designer, you must select the pattern for your future.

HERBERT KAUFMAN

Day 2

The Right Course

The whole course of things goes to teach us faith. We need only obey. There is guidance for each of us, and by lowly listening we shall hear the right word. . . . Place yourself in the middle of the stream of power and wisdom which animates all whom it floats, and you are without effort impelled to truth, to right, and a perfect contentment.

RALPH WALDO EMERSON

On Wings like Eagles

Even youths grow tired and weary, and young men stumble and fall; but those who hope in the Lord will renew their strength. They will soar on wings like eagles; they will run and not grow weary, they will walk and not be faint.

ISAIAH 40:30–31 NIV

DAY 4

An Impulse to Soar

One can never consent to creep when one has an impulse to soar. There are so many difficulties in the way, so many discouragements; but I kept on trying, knowing that perseverance and patience win in the end.

HELEN KELLER

Measure of True Success

A man should conceive of a legitimate purpose in his heart, and set out to accomplish it. . . . Even if he fails again and again to accomplish his purpose (as he necessarily must until weakness is overcome), the strength of character gained will be the measure of his true success, and this will form a new starting point for future power and triumph.

JAMES ALLEN

Day 6

Invincible Determination

An invincible determination can accomplish almost anything and in this lies the great distinction between great men and little men.

THOMAS FULLER

How to Succeed

If you wish to succeed in life,
make perseverance your bosom friend,
experience your wise counselor, caution your
elder brother, and hope your guardian genius.

JOSEPH ADDISON

DAY 8

Living in Truth

Only he who lives in truth finds it. The deepest truth is not born of conscious striving, but comes in the quiet hour when a noble nature gives itself into the keeping of life, to suffer, to feel, to think, and to act as it is moved by a wisdom not its own.

HAMILTON WRIGHT MABIE

Day 9

The Highest Activity

It is when the soul becomes utterly passive, looking and resting on what Christ is to do, that its energies are stirred to their highest activity, and that we work most effectually because we know that He works in us.

ANDREW MURRAY

Day 10

Determined Not to Quit

What this power is I cannot say; all I know is that it exists and it becomes available only when a man is in that state of mind in which he knows exactly what he wants and is fully determined not to quit until he finds it.

ALEXANDER GRAHAM BELL

Blazers of the Way

They are the chosen few—the Blazers of the Way—who never wear Doubt's bandage on their eyes—who starve and chill and hurt, but hold to courage and to hope, because they know that there is always proof of truth for them who try—that only cowardice and lack of faith can keep the seeker from his chosen goal.

HERBERT KAUFMAN

Day 12

Uniquely You

Every human being is intended to have a character of his own; to be what no others are, and to do what no other can do.

WILLIAM ELLERY CHANNING

Day 13

The Strength of Spiritual Force

Great men are they who see that spiritual is stronger than any material force, that thoughts rule the world.

RALPH WALDO EMERSON

Day 14

God's Roadmap

God has a plan for your life. To ensure you're on the right path, seek His face. Abide in His presence. Follow His direction. Don't take shortcuts. Obey the signs. And the road of life you travel will be paved with goodness only He can provide.

Great Aim

The important thing in life is to have a great aim, and to possess the aptitude and perseverance to attain it.

JOHANN WOLFGANG VON GOETHE

DAY 16

Divine Peace

In the very depths of yourself dig a grave. Let it be like some forgotten spot to which no path leads; and there, in the eternal silence, bury the wrongs that you have suffered. Your heart will feel as if a weight had fallen from it, and a divine peace will come to abide with you.

CHARLES WAGNER

The Waste of Life

Every year I live I am more convinced that the waste of life lies in the love we have not given, the powers we have not used, the selfish prudence which will risk nothing, and which, shirking pain, misses happiness as well.

MARY CHOLMONDELEY

Day 18

Be Resolved

We must not desire all to begin by perfection. It matters little how we begin, provided we be resolved to go on well and end well.

LELAND STANFORD

The Means of Prayer

The Divine wisdom has given us prayer, not as a means whereby to obtain the good things of earth, but as a means whereby we learn to do without them; not as a means whereby we escape evil, but as a means whereby we become strong to meet it.

FREDERICK WILLIAM ROBERTSON

DAY 20

Strive after Contentment

Let your strivings, then, be after contentment. Get out of each passing day all the sweetness there is in it. Live in the present hour as much as possible, and if you live for character your foundations will outlast tomorrow. It is when men build without moral principle that they need fear the future.

GEORGE H. HEPWORTH

Be Patterns

Be patterns, be examples in all countries, places, islands, nations, wherever you come; that your carriage and life may preach among all sorts of people and to them; then you will come to walk cheerfully over the world, answering that of God in everyone; whereby in them you may be a blessing, and make the witness of God in them to bless you.

GEORGE FOX

DAY 22

Spirit-Poured Dreams and Visions

"I will pour out my Spirit upon all people.
Your sons and daughters will prophesy.
Your old men will dream dreams, and your young men will see visions. In those days I will pour out my Spirit even on servants—men and women alike."

JOEL 2:28–29 NLT

Seedlings of Realities

The greatest achievement was at first and for a time a dream. The oak sleeps in the acorn; the bird waits in the egg; and in the highest vision of the soul a waking angel stirs. Dreams are the seedlings of realities.

JAMES ALLEN

DAY 24

Believe the Dream

Ah, great it is to believe the dream
As we stand in youth by starry stream;
But a greater thing it is to fight life through,
And say at the end, "The dream is true!"

EDWIN MARKHAM

Day 25

Solid Comfort

The most solid comfort one can fall back upon is the thought that the business of one's life. . .is to help in some small nibbling way to reduce the sum of ignorance, degradation, and misery on the face of this beautiful earth.

GEORGE ELIOT

Day 26

Without a Foundation

To scorn delights and live laborious days; to bind one's self to an unceasing and unchanging routine, as Ixion to his wheel, for the sake of amassing money that some time, in a dim and abstract future, one may begin to live, is simply to attempt building a superstructure without a foundation.

LILIAN WHITING

Find Your Niche

Find your niche and fill it. If it is ever so little, if it is only a hewer of wood or a drawer of water, do something in the great battle for God and truth.

CHARLES SPURGEON

DAY 28

The Ideal Life

The ideal life is in our blood and never will be still. Sad will be the day for any man when he becomes contented with the thoughts he is thinking and the deeds he is doing—where there is not forever beating at the doors of his soul some great desire to do something larger, which he knows that he was meant and made to do.

PHILLIPS BROOKS

Nothing So Small

There is nothing so small but that we may honor God by asking His guidance of it, or insult Him by taking it into our hands.

JOHN RUSKIN

Day 30

The Necessity of God

One person who has mastered life is better than a thousand persons who have mastered only the contents of books, but no one can get anything out of life without God.

MEISTER ECKHART

Keep Walking

If you would attain to what you are not yet, you must always be displeased by what you are. For where you are pleased with yourself there you have remained. Keep adding, keep walking, keep advancing.

SAINT AUGUSTINE

Day 32

You Can!

Do all the good you can,
By all the means you can,
In all the ways you can,
In all the places you can,
At all the times you can,
To all the people you can,
As long as ever you can.

JOHN WESLEY

Dare to Act

Dare to renew your decision. It will lift you up again to have trust in God. For God is a spirit of power and love and self-control, and it is before God and for him that every decision is to be made. Dare to act on the good that lies buried within your heart.

SOREN KIERKEGAARD

Day 34

Wonder

Wonder, connected with a principle of rational curiosity, is the source of all knowledge and discovery, and it is a principle even of piety; but wonder which ends in wonder, and is satisfied with wonder, is the quality of an idiot.

SAMUEL HORSLEY

Day 35

Gifted for Something

Life is not easy for any of us. But what of that? We must have perseverance and above all confidence in ourselves. We must believe that we are gifted for something and that this thing must be attained.

MARIE CURIE

Day 36

The Silent Power

There are two ways of attaining an important end, force and perseverance; the silent power of the latter grows irresistible with time.

ANNIE SOPHIE SWETCHINE

Believing the Unbelievable

To love means loving the unlovable. To forgive means pardoning the unpardonable.
Faith means believing the unbelievable. Hope means hoping when everything seems hopeless.

G. K. CHESTERTON

DAY 38

From Hope to Hope

The mind is never satisfied with the objects immediately before it, but is always breaking away from the present moment, and losing itself in schemes of future felicity. . . . The natural flights of the human mind are not from pleasure to pleasure, but from hope to hope.

SAMUEL JOHNSON

By Your Own Consent

No power in society, no hardship in your condition, can depress you, keep you down, in knowledge, power, virtue, influence, but by your own consent.

WILLIAM ELLERY CHANNING

Day 40

Firm Hearts

I love those who can smile in trouble, who can gather strength from distress, and grow brave by reflection. 'Tis the business of little minds to shrink, but they whose heart is firm, and whose conscience approves their conduct, will pursue their principles unto death.

LEONARDO DA VINCI

A Happening Comes

It is almost always when things are all blocked up and impossible, that a happening comes. It has to. A dead block can't last, any more than a vacuum. If you are sure you are looking and ready, that is all you need. God is turning the world round all the time.

MRS. A. T. D. WHITNEY

Day 42

What We Read

What we become depends on what we read after all of the professors have finished with us. The greatest university of all is a collection of books.

THOMAS CARLYLE

The Way to Life

"Don't look for shortcuts to God. The market is flooded with surefire, easygoing formulas for a successful life that can be practiced in your spare time. Don't fall for that stuff, even though crowds of people do. The way to life—to God!—is vigorous and requires total attention."

MATTHEW 7:13–14 MSG

Day 44

Great Progress

The soul seeks God by faith, not by the reasonings of the mind and labored efforts, but by the drawings of love; to which inclinations God responds, and instructs the soul, which co-operates actively. God then puts the soul in a passive state where He accomplishes all, causing great progress.

MADAME JEANNE GUYON

God-Shaped Vacuum

There is a God-shaped vacuum in the heart of every man which cannot be filled by any created thing, but only by God, the Creator, made known through Jesus.

BLAISE PASCAL

Day 46

Believe in What You Are Doing

If you want to be successful, it's just this simple. Know what you are doing. Love what you are doing. And believe in what you are doing.

WILL ROGERS

DAY 47

Thread in the Labyrinth

He who every morning plans the transactions of the day and follows that plan, carries a thread that will guide him through a labyrinth of the most busy life.

VICTOR HUGO

Day 48

Making Room

Depend upon it, there comes a time when for every addition of knowledge you forget something that you knew before. It is of the highest importance, therefore, not to have useless facts elbowing out the useful ones.

ARTHUR CONAN DOYLE

Bent on Making Dreams Come True

The ninety and nine are with dreams, content, but the hope of the world made new, is the hundredth man who is grimly bent on making those dreams come true.

EDGAR ALLEN POE

DAY 50

Because You Have Lived

To appreciate beauty; to find the best in others; to give of one's self; to leave the world a bit better . . .to have played and laughed with enthusiasm and sung with exultation; to know even one life has breathed easier because you have lived—this is to have succeeded.

RALPH WALDO EMERSON

Gift of Making Friends

Blessed are they who have the gift of making friends, for it is one of God's best gifts. It involves many things, but above all, the power of going out of one's self, and appreciating whatever is noble and loving in another.

THOMAS HUGHES

Day 52

An Outlet to Forces Within

Blessed is the man who has some congenial work, some occupation in which he can put his heart, and which affords a complete outlet to all the forces there are in him.

JOHN BURROUGHS

Fault Lines

Nothing will make us so charitable and tender to the faults of others, as, by self-examination, thoroughly to know our own.

FRANÇOIS FÉNELON

DAY 54

Vanity and Pride

Vanity and pride are different things, though the words are often used synonymously. A person may be proud without being vain. Pride relates more to our opinion of ourselves, vanity to what we would have others think of us.

JANE AUSTEN

Doing a Job Right

The world does not demand that you be a physician, a lawyer, a farmer, or a merchant; but it does demand that whatever you do undertake, you will do it right, will do it with all your might and with all the ability you possess. It demands that you be a master in your line.

ORISON SWETT MARDEN

DAY 56

What You Ought to Do

If you do not know what you ought to do, stand still until you do. And when the time comes for action, circumstances, like glowworms, will sparkle along your path; and you will become so sure that you are right, when God's three witnesses concur, that you could not be surer though an angel beckoned you on.

F. B. MEYER

Finding a Pearl

There is an electric fire in human nature tending to purify—so that among these human creatures there is continually some birth of new heroism. The pity is that we must wonder at it, as we should at finding a pearl in rubbish.

JOHN KEATS

Day 58

Change and Transformation

The way of the Creative works through change and transformation, so that each thing receives its true nature and destiny and comes into permanent accord with the Great Harmony: this is what furthers and what perseveres.

ALEXANDER POPE

The Inner and Outer Man

A man is not rightly conditioned until he is a happy, healthy, and prosperous being; and happiness, health, and prosperity are the result of a harmonious adjustment of the inner with the outer of the man with his surroundings.

JAMES ALLEN

Day 60

Life Lessons

Life is divided into three terms—that which was, which is, and which will be. Let us learn from the past to profit by the present, and from the present to live better in the future.

WILLIAM WORDSWORTH

God's Instrument

Lord, make me an instrument of Thy peace;
Where there is hatred, let me sow love;
Where there is injury, pardon;
Where there is doubt, faith;
Where there is despair, hope;
Where there is darkness, light;
Where there is sadness, joy.

ST. FRANCIS OF ASSISI

DAY 62

Singleness of Purpose

You can have anything you want—if you want it badly enough. You can be anything you want to be, do anything you set out to accomplish if you hold to that desire with singleness of purpose.

ABRAHAM LINCOLN

No Wavering

Ask in faith, nothing wavering. For he that wavereth is like a wave of the sea driven with the wind and tossed. For let not that man think that he shall receive any thing of the Lord. A double minded man is unstable in all his ways.

JAMES 1:6–8 KJV

Laying a Course

No man has earned the right to intellectual ambition until he has learned to lay his course by a star that he has never seen—to dig by the divining rod for springs which he may never reach. . . . Only when you have worked alone. . .and in hope and in despair have trusted to your own [God-given] unshaken will—then only will you have achieved.

OLIVER WENDELL HOLMES

To Reach the Unreachable Stars

And I know, if I'll only be true
To this glorious quest,
That my heart will lie peaceful and calm
When I'm laid to my rest.
And the world will be better for this,
That one man scorned and covered with scars,
Still strove, with his last ounce of courage,
To reach the unreachable star!

JOE DARION

Day 66

Enough Happiness

Man is fond of counting his troubles, but he does not count his joys. If he counted them up as he ought to, he would see that every lot has enough happiness provided for it.

FYODOR DOSTOEVSKY

God's Infinite Patience

God is nearest to us, seeking us with an intensity of which our own longing for God is but a pale reflection. If we cannot at once open our souls to God's love and grace, let us in patience wait for God; and we shall discover at last that it is God who has been infinitely patient with us.

EDWARD GRUBB

Day 68

The Passing of Time

Time, as is well known, sometimes flies like a bird and sometimes crawls like a worm, but human beings are generally particularly happy when they don't notice whether it's passing quickly or slowly.

IVAN TURGENEV

The Great Chewing Complacency

Don't let your special character and values, the secret that you know and no one else does, the truth—don't let that get swallowed up by the great chewing complacency.

AESOP

Day 70

Wants and Means

There are two ways of being happy: We must either diminish our wants or augment our means—either may do—the result is the same and it is for each man to decide for himself and to do that which happens to be easier.

BENJAMIN FRANKLIN

True to Myself

I prefer to be true to myself, even at the hazard of incurring the ridicule of others, rather than to be false, and to incur my own abhorrence.

FREDERICK DOUGLASS

Secure Within

Happy the man, and happy he alone,
He who can call today his own:
He who, secure within, can say,
Tomorrow do thy worst, for I have lived today.

JOHN DRYDEN

A Noble Ideal

He who, having lost one ideal, refuses to give his heart and soul to another and nobler, is like a man who declines to build a house on rock because the wind and rain ruined his house on the sand.

CONSTANCE NADEN

DAY 74

Of Immense Importance

When we can begin to take our failures seriously, it means we are ceasing to be afraid of them. It is of immense importance to learn to laugh at ourselves.

KATHERINE MANSFIELD

Restored One Hundredfold

They who are God's without reserve, are in every state content; for they will only what He wills, and desire to do for Him whatever He desires them to do; they strip themselves of everything, and in this nakedness find all things restored an hundredfold.

CHARLES SPURGEON

Day 76

Straighter Paths

Like a morning dream, life becomes more and more bright the longer we live, and the reason of everything appears more clear. What has puzzled us before seems less mysterious, and the crooked paths look straighter as we approach the end.

JEAN PAUL RICHTER

Potential for Success

Success consists in being successful, not in having potential for success. Any wide piece of ground is the potential site of a palace, but there's no palace till it's built.

FERNANDO PESSOA

Day 78

Essential Solitude

Solitude, though it may be silent as light, is like light, the mightiest of agencies; for solitude is essential to man. All men come into this world alone and leave it alone.

THOMAS DE QUINCEY

Natural Recreation

Walking is the natural recreation for a man who desires not absolutely to suppress his intellect but to turn it out to play for a season. All great men of letters have therefore been enthusiastic walkers.

LESLIE STEPHEN

DAY 80

Regrets Only

Regret the days you lose, the hours you fritter away; regret the speech that wounded, the unjust suspicion, the hasty judgment. But never regret that you followed your heart when it led you toward confidence, toward sincerity, toward kindness.

CHARLES WAGNER

Hope!

Ah, Hope! what would life be, stripped of thy encouraging smiles, that teach us to look behind the dark clouds of today, for the golden beams that are to gild the morrow.

SUSANNA MOODIE

DAY 82

Great in Little Things

To be really great in little things, to be truly noble and heroic in the insipid details of everyday life, is a virtue so rare as to be worthy of canonization.

HARRIET BEECHER STOWE

A Life Worthy

I urge you to live a life worthy of the calling you have received. Be completely humble and gentle; be patient, bearing with one another in love. Make every effort to keep the unity of the Spirit through the bond of peace.

EPHESIANS 4:1–3 NIV

DAY 84

A Tender Hand

Our life is love, and peace, and tenderness; and bearing one with another, and forgiving one another, and not laying accusations one against another; but praying for one another, and helping one another up with a tender hand.

ISAAC PENINGTON

Finding the Lovable

The task is not to find the lovable object, but to find the object before you lovable—whether given or chosen—and to be able to continue finding this one lovable, no matter how that person changes. To love is to love the person one *sees.*

SOREN KIERKEGAARD

Day 86

Adding Our Mite to the Future

I am an enthusiast, but not a crank in the sense that I have some pet theories as to the proper construction of a flying machine. I wish to avail myself of all that is already known and then, if possible, add my mite to help on the future worker who will attain final success.

WILBUR WRIGHT

Fight-to-the-Finish Spirit

All endeavor calls for the ability to tramp the last mile, shape the last plan, endure the last hours toil. The fight to the finish spirit is the one. . .characteristic we must posses if we are to face the future as finishers.

HENRY DAVID THOREAU

Day 88

The Few and Far Between

The average person puts only 25 percent of his energy and ability into his work. The world takes off its hat to those who put in more than 50 percent of their capacity, and stands on its head for those few and far between souls who devote 100 percent.

ANDREW CARNEGIE

Working Unerringly

The point is not to take the world's opinion as a guiding star but to go one's way in life and working unerringly, neither depressed by failure nor seduced by applause.

GUSTAV MAHLER

DAY 90

Real Effort

Remember the sufferings of Christ, the storms that were weathered. . .the crown that came from those sufferings which gave new radiance to the faith. . . . All saints give testimony to the truth that without real effort, no one ever wins the crown.

THOMAS BECKET

The Folly of Worrying

Early in my business career I learned the folly of worrying about anything. I have always worked as hard as I could, but when a thing went wrong and could not be righted, I dismissed it from my mind.

JULIUS ROSENWALD

Apprehension—No Limits

Grief has limits, whereas apprehension has none. For we grieve only for what we know has happened, but we fear all that possibly may happen.

PLINY THE ELDER

The Handle of Faith

Every tomorrow has two handles. We can take hold of it with the handle of anxiety or the handle of faith.

HENRY WARD BEECHER

Day 94

Feeding the Mind

The mind, in proportion as it is cut off from free communication with nature, with revelation, with God, with itself, loses its life, just as the body droops when debarred from the air and the cheering light from heaven.

WILLIAM ELLERY CHANNING

Day 95

Employed in Divine Thoughts

When you cease from labour, fill up your time in reading, meditation, and prayer: and while your hands are labouring, let your heart be employed, as much as possible, in divine thoughts.

DAVID BRAINERD

The Key to Good Health

Never hurry. Take plenty of exercise. Always be cheerful. Take all the sleep you need. You may expect to be well.

JAMES FREEMAN CLARKE

The Benefits of Responsibility

Responsibility is the thing people dread most of all. Yet it is the one thing in the world that develops us, gives us manhood or womanhood fiber.

FRANK CRANE

DAY 98

The Power of Teamwork

As long as a house is like yours, and as long as you work together with your brothers, not a house in the world will be able to compete with you, to cause you harm or to take advantage of you, for together you can undertake and perform more than any house in the world.

NATHAN MEYER ROTHSCHILD

Day 99

The Value of a Friend

A friend should be one in whose understanding and virtue we can equally confide, and whose opinion we can value at once for its justness and its sincerity.

ROBERT HALL

Day 100

Creative Power

Dreaming is an act of pure imagination, attesting in all men a creative power, which if it were available in waking, would make every man a Dante or Shakespeare.

FREDERICK HENRY HEDGE

The Danger of Doubt

A person who doubts himself is like a man who would enlist in the ranks of his enemies and bear arms against himself. He makes his failure certain by himself being the first person to be convinced of it.

AMBROSE BIERCE

The Key to Every Situation

Man is made or unmade by himself. By the right choice he ascends. As a being of power, intelligence, and love, and the lord of his own thoughts, he holds the key to every situation.

JAMES ALLEN

Every Good Purpose

With this in mind, we constantly pray for you, that our God may count you worthy of his calling, and that by his power he may fulfill every good purpose of yours and every act prompted by your faith.

2 THESSALONIANS 1:11 NIV

Day 104

But One Master

A servant of God has but one Master. It ill becomes the servant to seek to be rich, and great, and honored in that world where his Lord was poor, and mean, and despised.

GEORGE MÜLLER

A Latent Force

Without passion man is a mere latent force and possibility, like the flint which awaits the shock of the iron before it can give forth its spark.

HENRI FREDERIC AMIEL

When the Time Calls

Because just as arms have no force outside if there is no counsel within a house, study is vain and counsel useless that is not put to virtuous effect when the time calls.

FRANÇOIS RABELAIS

Standing the Test

Do something everyday for no other reason than you would rather not do it, so that when the hour of dire need draws nigh, it may find you not unnerved and untrained to stand the test.

WILLIAM JAMES

Day 108

Uttermost Love

God is stronger than their strength, more loving than their uttermost love, and in so far as they have loved and sacrificed themselves for others, they have obtained the infallible proof, that God too lives and loves and gives Himself away.

GEORGE A. SMITH

But One Motive

We acknowledge but one motive to follow the truth as we know it, whithersoever it may lead us; but in our heart of hearts we are well assured that the truth which has made us free, will in the end make us glad also.

MORTIMER ADLER

Divine Services of a Conviction

Broad paths are open to every endeavour, and a sympathetic recognition is assured to every one who consecrates his art to the divine services of a conviction of a consciousness.

FRANZ LISZT

The Steps of a Good Man

We often make a great mistake, thinking that God is not guiding us at all, because we cannot see far in front. But this is not His method. He only undertakes that the steps of a good man should be ordered by the Lord. Not next year, but tomorrow. Not the next mile, but the next yard.

F. B. MEYER

Day 112

Our Divine Pilot

Seeing that a Pilot steers the ship in which we sail, who will never allow us to perish even in the midst of shipwrecks, there is no reason why our minds should be overwhelmed with fear and overcome with weariness.

JOHN CALVIN

The Hundred and First Blow

I'd look at one of my stonecutters hammering away at the rock, perhaps a hundred times without as much as a crack showing in it. Yet, at the hundred and first blow it would split in two, and I knew it was not that blow that did it, but all that had gone before.

JACOB AUGUST RIIS

Day 114

The Hallmark of a Transition

You might feel both helpless and hopeless without a sense of a "map" for the journey. Confusion is the hallmark of a transition. To rebuild both your inner and outer world is a major project.

ANNE GRANT

The Importance of Enthusiasm

Nobody grows old merely by living a number of years. We grow old by deserting our ideals. Years may wrinkle the skin, but to give up enthusiasm wrinkles the soul. Worry, fear, self-distrust bows the heart and turns the spirit back to dust.

SAMUEL ULLMAN

Day 116

The Gift of Conversation

The great gift of conversation lies less in displaying it ourselves than in drawing it out of others. He who leaves your company pleased with himself and his own cleverness is perfectly well pleased with you.

JEAN DE LA BRUYÈRE

The Blessing of a Friend

A blessed thing it is for any man or woman to have a friend, one human soul whom we can trust utterly, who knows the best and worst of us, and who loves us in spite of all our faults.

CHARLES KINGSLEY

A First Effort

A great deal of talent is lost to the world for want of a little courage. Every day sends to their graves obscure men whose timidity prevented them from making a first effort.

SYDNEY SMITH

Getting Through

If you've ever been in a position in your life where you just can't take any more, you just have to get through the next second, and the next second after that.

MICHAEL NOVAK

Day 120

Endeavor to Be Faithful

Endeavour to be faithful, and if there is any beauty in your thought, your style will be beautiful; if there is any real emotion to express, the expression will be moving.

GEORGE HENRY LEWES

Swing the Door Wide Open

Get into the habit of dealing with God about everything. Unless in the first waking moment of the day you learn to fling the door wide back and let God in, you will work on a wrong level all day; but swing the door wide open and pray to your Father in secret, and every public thing will be stamped with the presence of God.

OSWALD CHAMBERS

Day 122

The Praying Soul

Never was a faithful prayer lost. Some prayers have a longer voyage than others, but then they return with their richer lading at last, so that the praying soul is a gainer by waiting for an answer.

WILLIAM GURNALL

Rewards of Diligence

Now faith is the substance of things hoped for, the evidence of things not seen. But without faith it is impossible to please Him, for he who comes to God must believe that He is, and that He is a rewarder of those who diligently seek Him.

HEBREWS 11:1, 6 NKJV

DAY 124

To Be an Artist

To be an artist includes much; one must possess many gifts, absolute gifts which have not been acquired by one's own effort. And, moreover, to succeed, the artist must possess the courageous soul.

KATE CHOPIN

God's Servants

We should always look upon ourselves as God's servants, placed in God's world, to do his work; and accordingly labour faithfully for him; not with a design to grow rich and great, but to glorify God, and do all the good we possibly can.

DAVID BRAINERD

Day 126

Liberty to Be

The real democratic American idea is, not that every man shall be on a level with every other man, but that every man shall have liberty to be what God made him, without hindrance.

HENRY WARD BEECHER

Less of Our Selves

Sensitiveness is closely allied to egotism; and excessive sensibility is only another name for morbid self-consciousness. The cure for tender sensibilities is to make more of our objects and less of our selves.

CHRISTIAN NESTELL BOVEE

Day 128

The Use of Our Days

The value of life lies not in the length of days, but in the use we make of them. . . . Whether you find satisfaction in life depends not on your tale of years, but on your will.

MICHEL DE MONTAIGNE

The Best Books

The best books for a man are not always those which the wise recommend, but often those which meet the peculiar wants, the natural thirst of his mind, and therefore awaken interest and rivet thought.

WILLIAM ELLERY CHANNING

A Single Occupation

All things will be produced in superior quantity and quality, and with greater ease, when each man works at a single occupation, in accordance with his natural gifts, and at the right moment, without meddling with anything else.

PLATO

The Important Thing

A road well begun is the battle half won.
The important thing is to make a beginning and get under way. There is nothing more harmful for your soul than to hold back and not get moving. . . . In the end, the archenemy of decision is cowardice.

SOREN KIERKEGAARD

Day 132

The Importance of "Other Things"

There is a serious defect in the thinking of someone who wants—more than anything else—to become rich. As long as they don't have the money, it'll seem like a worthwhile goal. Once they do, they'll understand how important other things are—and have always been.

BENJAMIN JOWETT

Great Thoughts and Good Deeds

Let each man think himself an act of God, his mind a thought, his life a breath of God; and let each try, by great thoughts and good deeds, to show the most of Heaven he hath in him.

PHILIP JAMES BAILEY

DAY 134

The Mind and Will of God

Those of you who can read I must beg you to read the Bible, and whenever you can get time, study the Bible, and if you can get no other time, spare some of your time from sleep, and learn what the mind and will of God is.

JUPITER HAMMON

Attention to the Small Things

Success in life is founded upon attention to the small things rather than to the large things; to the every day things nearest to us rather than to the things that are remote and uncommon.

BOOKER T. WASHINGTON

Day 136

Dreams of Lofty Purpose

But we can hold our spirits and our bodies so pure and high, we may cherish such thoughts and such ideals, and dream such dreams of lofty purpose, that we can determine and know what manner of men we will be, whenever and wherever the hour strikes and calls to noble action.

JOSHUA CHAMBERLAIN

Transforming Power

The maturity of a Christian experience cannot be reached in a moment, but is the result of the work of God's Holy Spirit, who, by His energizing and transforming power, causes us to grow up into Christ in all things. And we cannot hope to reach this maturity in any other way, than by yielding ourselves up, utterly and willingly, to His mighty working.

HANNAH WHITALL SMITH

Day 138

The Vision of the Hero

The prudent see only the difficulties, the bold only the advantages, of a great enterprise; the hero sees both; diminishes the former and makes the latter preponderate, and so conquers.

JOHANN KASPAR LAVATER

God's Providential Arrangement

It is not by regretting what is irreparable that true work is to be done, but by making the best of what we are. It is not by complaining that we have not the right tools, but by using well the tools we have. What we are, and where we are, is God's providential arrangement.

FREDERICK WILLIAM ROBERTSON

DAY 140

What You Were Meant to Be

If the people about you are carrying on their business or their benevolence at a pace which drains the life out of you, resolutely take a slower pace, be called a laggard, make less money, accomplish less work than they, but be what you were meant to be and can be.

GEORGE S. MERRIAM

Try What Love Will Do

Let us then try what Love will do: For if Men did once see we Love them we should soon find they would not harm us. Force may subdue, but Love gains.

WILLIAM PENN

Day 142

Doing Something Else

Life is pretty simple: You do some stuff. Most fails. Some works. You do more of what works. If it works big, others quickly copy it. Then you do something else. The trick is the doing something else.

LEONARDO DA VINCI

Traveling by Faith

By an act of faith, Abraham said yes to God's call to travel to an unknown place that would become his home. When he left he had no idea where he was going. Abraham did it by keeping his eye on an unseen city with real, eternal foundations—the City designed and built by God.

HEBREWS 11:8, 10 MSG

DAY 144

A Deep Mental Path

As a single footstep will not make a path on the earth, so a single thought will not make a pathway in the mind. To make a deep physical path, we walk again and again. To make a deep mental path, we must think over and over the kind of thoughts we wish to dominate our lives.

HENRY DAVID THOREAU

Every Person Is God's Work

We must never undervalue any person. The workman loves not that his work should be despised in his presence. Now God is present everywhere, and every person is His work.

FRANCIS DE SALES

Day 146

On God's Anvil

Iron till it be thoroughly heated is incapable to be wrought; so God sees good to cast some men into the furnace of affliction, and then beats them on his anvil into what frame he pleases.

ANNE BRADSTREET

Get Up and Begin Again

But what if I fail of my purpose here? It is but to keep the nerves at strain, to dry one's eyes and laugh at a fall, and baffled, get up and begin again.

ROBERT BROWNING

Day 148

The Revelation of Crisis

Great occasions do not make heroes or cowards; they simply unveil them to the eyes of men. Silently and imperceptibly, as we wake or sleep, we grow strong or weak; and at last some crisis shows what we have become.

BROOKE FOSS WESTCOTT

Start Where You Stand

Do not wait; the time will never be "just right."
Start where you stand, and work with whatever
tools you may have at your command,
and better tools will be found as you go along.

GEORGE HERBERT

Day 150

Two Good Rules

There are two good rules which ought to be written on every heart—never to believe anything bad about anybody unless you positively know it to be true; never to tell even that unless you feel that it is absolutely necessary, and that God is listening.

HENRY VAN DYKE

The World of Beauty

Do not try to push your way through to the front ranks of your profession; do not run after distinctions and rewards; but do your utmost to find an entry into the world of beauty.

SYDNEY SMITH

Conveyed by Music

Though everything else may appear shallow and repulsive, even the smallest task in music is so absorbing, and carries us so far away from town, country, earth, and all worldly things, that it is truly a blessed gift of God.

FELIX MENDELSSOHN

Some Single Turning of the Soul

Happiness, contentment, the health and growth of the soul, depend, as men have proved over and over again, upon some simple issue, some single turning of the soul.

GEORGE A. SMITH

Day 154

Praying for a Miracle

Whatever a person may pray for, that person prays for a miracle. Every prayer comes down to this—Almighty God, grant that two times two not equal four.

IVAN TURGENEV

The Strength for Striving

The relationship to one's fellow man is the relationship of prayer, the relationship to oneself is the relationship of striving; it is from prayer that one draws the strength for one's striving.

FRANZ KAFKA

What I Can Do

I am only one, but I am one. I cannot do everything, but I can do something. And I will not let what I cannot do interfere with what I can do.

EDWARD EVERETT HALE

To Study and to Do

The atmosphere is much too near for dreams. It forces us to action. It is close to us. We are in it and of it. It rouses us both to study and to do. We must know its moods and also its motive forces.

CLEVELAND ABBE

Abide in Peace

Accustom yourself to unreasonableness and injustice. Abide in peace in the bosom of God, who sees all these evils more clearly than you do, and who permits them. Be content with doing without excitement the little which depends on you, and let all else be to you as if it were not.

FRANÇOIS FÉNELON

The Rule of Forgiveness

He that cannot forgive others breaks the bridge over which he must pass himself; for every man has need to be forgiven.

THOMAS FULLER

DAY 160

Our Happiness

It is a great truth, wonderful as it is undeniable, that all our happiness—temporal, spiritual, and eternal—consists in one thing; namely, in resigning ourselves to God, and in leaving ourselves with Him, to do with us and in us just as He pleases.

MADAME JEANNE GUYON

A Healthy State of Mind

Your very health depends largely on your state of mind, and when your mind has soared to that realm in which your God dwells, not only does your body respond, but your whole outlook undergoes a change.

GEORGE H. HEPWORTH

Day 162

The Talent of Success

The talent of success is nothing more than doing what you can do well, and doing well whatever you do without thought of fame. If it comes at all it will come because it is deserved, not because it is sought after.

HENRY WADSWORTH LONGFELLOW

Five Talents

" 'Master,' he said, 'you entrusted me with five talents. See, I have gained five more.'

"His master replied, 'Well done, good and faithful servant! You have been faithful with a few things; I will put you in charge of many things. Come and share your master's happiness!' "

MATTHEW 25:20–21 NIV

Powers and Faculties

If we desire real happiness, we have no other possible way to it, but by improving our talents, by so holily and piously using the powers and faculties of men in this present state, that we may be happy and glorious in the powers and faculties of angels in the world to come.

WILLIAM LAW

Among the Angels

Your enjoyment of the world is never right,
till every morning you awake in Heaven:
see yourself in your Father's palace;
and look upon the skies, the earth, and the
air as celestial joys: having such a reverend
esteem of all, as if you were among the
angels.

THOMAS TRAHERNE

DAY 166

A Sustaining Hand

Let us lift up our hearts and ask, "Lord, what wouldest Thou have me to do?" Then light from the opened heaven shall stream on our daily task, revealing the grains of gold where yesterday all seemed dust; a Hand shall sustain us and our daily burden, so that smiling at yesterday's fears, we shall say, "This is easy, this is light."

ELIZABETH RUNDELL CHARLES

Hindrances to Work

Look on all interruptions and hindrances to work that one has planned out for oneself as discipline, trials sent by God. . . . After such a hindrance, do not rush after the planned work, trust that the time to finish it well will be given some time, and keep a quiet heart about it.

ANNIE KEARY

The Flower of Desire

Hope may be described as the flower of desire. It expects that the object shall be attained. It bars despondence and anticipates good. It shakes the mind from stagnation, animates to encounter danger, and is the balm of life. Though at times it may be associated with doubt and solicitude, yet when hesitance is displaced, it swells into joy and ecstasy.

THEODORE LEDYARD CUYLER

Let Nothing Escape Us

Half the joy of life is in little things taken on the run. . .but let us keep our hearts young and our eyes open that nothing worth our while shall escape us.

C. VICTOR CHERBULIEZ

Day 170

Inward Peace

Those that make God their hope, they shall flourish in credit and comfort, like a tree that is always green, whose leaf does not wither; they shall be cheerful to themselves and beautiful in the eyes of others. . . . They shall be fixed in an inward peace and satisfaction.

MATTHEW HENRY

The Presence of God

By the presence of God being with us, it is known to ourselves, and to others what we are. . . . They are then best known to themselves. They know they are his people, because God's presence is with them. Therefore he saith, "My presence shall go with thee, and I will give thee rest."

JOHN BUNYAN

DAY 172

At the Heart of Things

Let us be at peace, because peace is at the heart of things—peace and utter satisfaction between the Father and the Son—in which peace they call us to share; in which peace they promise that at length, when they have their good way with us, we shall share.

GEORGE MACDONALD

Worthy of General Discovery

When you awaken some morning and hear that somebody or other has been discovered, you can put it down as a fact that he discovered himself years ago—since that time he has been toiling, working, and striving to make himself worthy of general discovery.

JAMES WHITCOMB RILEY

DAY 174

The Tide Will Turn

When you get into a tight place and everything goes against you, till it seems as though you could not hang on a minute longer, never give up then, for that is just the place and time that the tide will turn.

HARRIET BEECHER STOWE

Our Better Selves

When from our better selves we have too long been parted by the hurrying world, and droop. Sick of its business, of its pleasures tired, how gracious, how benign in solitude.

WILLIAM WORDSWORTH

Day 176

Fixing Our Attention

Every year of my life I grow more convinced that it is wisest and best to fix our attention on the beautiful and the good, and dwell as little as possible on the evil and the false.

RICHARD CECIL

The Great Doers—People of Faith

Skepticism has never founded empires, established principals, or changed the world's heart. The great doers in history have always been people of faith.

EDWIN HUBBEL CHAPIN

Day 178

Ranks of Humanity

When we contemplate the heroes of Christianity, and compare our feeble efforts with their astonishing performance and self devotion, we should fall into despair, were there not a few softening features, by which they are brought back to the ranks of humanity.

JOHN STRACHAN

Wisdom and Knowledge

Wisdom is the right use of knowledge. To know is not to be wise. Many men know a great deal, and are all the greater fools for it. There is no fool so great a fool as a knowing fool. But to know how to use knowledge is to have wisdom.

CHARLES SPURGEON

Sleep—the Universal Currency

Bless the man who invented sleep, a cloak to cover over all human thought, food that drives away hunger, water that banishes thirst, fire that heats up cold, chill that moderates passion, and, finally, universal currency with which all things can be bought, weight and balance that brings the shepherd and the king, the fool and the wise, to the same level.

MIGUEL DE CERVANTES

An Engaged Human Life

To be educated, a person doesn't have to know much or be informed, but he or she does have to have been exposed vulnerably to the transformative events of an engaged human life.

THOMAS MORE

No Limits

God will crown your endeavors with equal measures of that reward which he indeed freely gives, but yet gives according to our proportions. . . . Let your hope be patient, without tediousness of spirit, or hastiness of prefixing time. Make no limits or prescriptions to God; but let your prayers and endeavors go on still with a constant attendance on the periods of God's providence. . . . Go on still in hoping.

JEREMY TAYLOR

Pray for Anything

Then Jesus told them, "I tell you the truth, if you have faith and don't doubt, you can do things like this and much more. You can even say to this mountain, 'May you be lifted up and thrown into the sea,' and it will happen. You can pray for anything, and if you have faith, you will receive it."

MATTHEW 21:21–22 NLT

DAY 184

Rise Like a Fountain

More things are wrought by prayer
than this world dreams of. Wherefore, let thy voice
rise like a fountain for me night and day.
For what are men better than sheep or goats
that nourish a blind life within the brain,
if, knowing God, they lift not hands of prayer
both for themselves and those who call them friend?

ALFRED LORD TENNYSON

Patiently Waiting

If honest of heart and uprightness before God were lacking or if I did not patiently wait on God for instruction, or if I preferred the counsel of my fellow-men to the declarations of the Word of God, I made great mistakes.

GEORGE MÜLLER

Visible and Invisible Labor

One is not idle because one is absorbed. There is both visible and invisible labor. To contemplate is to toil, to think is to do. The crossed arms work, the clasped hands act. The eyes upturned to Heaven are an act of creation.

VICTOR HUGO

The Gold of Real Service

For anything worth having one must pay the price; and the price is always work, patience, love, self-sacrifice—no paper currency, no promises to pay, but the gold of real service.

JOHN BURROUGHS

Making Headway

If you are steadfast and respect your tools, if you care enough and dare enough, you'll make headway anywhere and at anything.

HERBERT KAUFMAN

Little, Soon-Forgotten Charities

The happiness of life, on the contrary, is made up of minute fractions—the little, soon-forgotten charities of a kiss, a smile, a kind look, a heartfelt compliment.

SAMUEL TAYLOR COLERIDGE

DAY 190

A Life of Infinite Value

It is not the smallness of your life, but the quality of it, that is important. You cannot be an oak or an elm, but if you are a violet under a maple, drinking in the sunshine and the dew; you should be content, for in the providence of God humble lives cheerfully lived have infinite value.

GEORGE H. HEPWORTH

Because I Love

Love is life. All, everything that I understand, I understand only because I love. Everything is, everything exists, only because I love. Everything is united by it alone. Love is God.

LEO TOLSTOY

Day 192

Success Unexpected

I have learned, that if one advances confidently in the direction of his dreams, and endeavors to live the life he has imagined, he will meet with a success unexpected in common hours.

HENRY DAVID THOREAU

Singular Service

I have a secret thought from some things I have observed, that God may perhaps design you for some singular service in the world.

DAVID BRAINERD

Day 194

The Foundation of Wisdom

The most excellent and divine counsel, the best and most profitable advertisement of all others, but the least practiced, is to study and learn how to know ourselves. This is the foundation of wisdom and the highway to whatever is good.

PIERRE CHARRON

Turing Dreams into Reality

There are some people who live in a dream world, and there are some who face reality; and then there are those who turn one into the other.

DESIDERIUS ERASMUS

Day 196

Cases of Confidence

Attempt easy tasks as if they were difficult, and difficult as if they were easy; in the one case that confidence may not fall asleep, in the other that it may not be dismayed.

BALTASAR GRACIAN

Promises and Messages

The dreams which reveal the supernatural are promises and messages that God sends us directly: they are nothing but His angels, His ministering spirits, who usually appear to us when we are in a great predicament.

PARACELSUS

DAY 198

Revelations

When I was young I was sure of everything; in a few years, having been mistaken a thousand times, I was not half so sure of most things as I was before; at present, I am hardly sure of anything but what God has revealed to me.

JOHN WESLEY

Master of Himself

A man has to learn that he cannot command things, but that he can command himself; that he cannot coerce the wills of others, but that he can mold and master his own will: and things serve him who serves Truth; people seek guidance of him who is master of himself.

JAMES ALLEN

Promised Grace

God does not give grace till the hour of trial comes. But when it does come, the amount of grace and the special grace required is vouchsafed. My soul, do not dwell with painful apprehensions on the future. Do not anticipate coming sorrows; perplexing thyself about the grace needed for future emergencies: tomorrow will bring its promised grace along with tomorrow's trials.

JOHN MACDUFF

Claim Victory!

Only be strong and very courageous! Fear not, nor be dismayed! The Lord is with you, O mighty men of valor—mighty because you are one with the Mightiest. Claim victory! Whenever your enemies close in upon you, claim victory! Whenever heart and flesh fail, look up and claim Victory!

F. B. MEYER

DAY 202

Be the Miracle

Do not pray for easy lives. Pray to be stronger men. Do not pray for tasks equal to your powers. Pray for powers equal to your tasks. Then the doing of your work shall be no miracle, but you shall be the miracle.

PHILLIPS BROOKS

Even Greater Things

"Believe me when I say that I am in the Father and the Father is in me; or at least believe on the evidence of the miracles themselves. . . . Anyone who has faith in me will do what I have been doing. He will do even greater things than these."

JOHN 14:11–12 NIV

DAY 204

Appropriated Promises

[God] then gave me many other promises. . . . They did not seem so much to fall into my intellect as into my heart, to be put within the grasp of the voluntary powers of my mind; and I seized hold of them, appropriated them, and fastened upon them with the grasp of a drowning man.

CHARLES FINNEY

Your Heart's Desire

If your desire and aim is to reach the destination of the path and home of true happiness, of grace and glory, by a straight and safe way then earnestly apply your mind to seek constant purity of heart, clarity of mind and calm of the senses. Gather up your heart's desire and fix it continually on the Lord God above.

ALBERT THE GREAT

DAY 206

A Magnificent Victory

"But David encouraged himself in the Lord his God"; and the result was a magnificent victory. . . . He turns at once to the Lord, and by faith begins to praise Him. It is the only way. Discouragement flies where faith appears; and, vice versa, faith flies when discouragement appears. We must choose between them, for they will not mix.

HANNAH WHITALL SMITH

Light Within

He that has light within his own clear breast
May sit in the centre, and enjoy bright day:
But he that hides a dark soul and foul thoughts
Benighted walks under the mid-day sun;
Himself is his own dungeon.

JOHN MILTON

True Godliness

True godliness does not turn men out of the world, but enables them to live better in it, and excites their endeavors to mend it: not hide their candle under a bushel, but set it upon a table in a candlestick.

WILLIAM PENN

Perplexity of Life

The perplexity of life arises from there being too many interesting things in it for us to be interested properly in any of them.

G. K. CHESTERTON

DAY 210

Transfigured to a Blessing

Worry is a state of spiritual corrosion. A trouble either can be remedied, or it cannot. If it can be, then set about it; if it cannot be, dismiss it from consciousness, or bear it so bravely that it may become transfigured to a blessing.

LILIAN WHITING

Hidden as a Seed

Education is not the piling on of learning, information, data, facts, skills, or abilities—that's training or instruction—but is rather making visible what is hidden as a seed.

THOMAS MORE

DAY 212

Three Kinds of Trouble

Never bear more than one kind of trouble at a time. Some people bear three kinds of trouble—the ones they've had, the ones they have, and the ones they expect to have.

EDWARD EVERETT HALE

Poverty

Resolve not to be poor: whatever you have, spend less. Poverty is a great enemy to human happiness; it certainly destroys liberty, and it makes some virtues impracticable, and others extremely difficult.

SAMUEL JOHNSON

DAY 214

Greatness of Soul

He that can heroically endure adversity will bear prosperity with equal greatness of soul; for the mind that cannot be dejected by the former is not likely to be transported with the latter.

HENRY FIELDING

The Strength of Habit

Any act often repeated soon forms a habit; and habit allowed, steady gains in strength. At first it may be but as a spider's web, easily broken through, but if not resisted it soon binds us with chains of steel.

TRYON EDWARDS

DAY 216

Fear Less

Nothing in life is to be feared, it is only to be understood. Now is the time to understand more, so that we may fear less.

MARIE CURIE

Diligence

Diligence is the mother of good fortune, and idleness, its opposite, never brought a man to the goal of any of his best wishes.

MIGUEL DE CERVANTES

Day 218

What Was Lived and Lost

To feel today what one felt yesterday isn't to feel—it's to remember today what was felt yesterday, to be today's living corpse of what yesterday was lived and lost.

FERNANDO PESSOA

Another Happiness

All people desire what they believe will make them happy. If a person is not full of desire for God, we can only conclude that he is engaged with another happiness.

WILLIAM LAW

Day 220

Amid Your Occupations

Nothing else is required than to act toward God, in the midst of your occupations, as you do, even when busy, toward those who love you and whom you love.

ALPHONSUS LIGUORI

Jump In!

To do anything in this world worth doing, we must not stand back shivering and thinking of the cold and danger, but jump in and scramble through as well as we can. . . . Whatever you are by nature, keep to it; never desert your line of talent. Be what nature intended you for, and you will succeed.

SYDNEY SMITH

Sufficient for the Day

Banish the future. Live only for the hour and its allotted work. Think not of the amount to be accomplished, the difficulties to be overcome, or the end to be attained, but set earnestly at the little task at your elbow, letting that be sufficient for the day.

WILLIAM OSLER

God Will Help You Deal

"Give your entire attention to what God is doing right now, and don't get worked up about what may or may not happen tomorrow. God will help you deal with whatever hard things come up when the time comes."

MATTHEW 6:34 MSG

DAY 224

Never Be Ashamed

A man should never be ashamed to own he has been in the wrong, which is but saying, in other words, that he is wiser today than he was yesterday.

ALEXANDER POPE

When Cherished Schemes Fail

In war as in life, it is often necessary when some cherished scheme has failed, to take up the best alternative open, and if so, it is folly not to work for it with all your might.

WINSTON CHURCHILL

Day 226

Taking Responsibility

People without firmness of character love to make up a fate for themselves; that relieves them of the necessity of having their own will and of taking responsibility for themselves.

IVAN TURGENEV

An Important Imagination

To think the world therefore a general Bedlam, or place of madmen, and oneself a physician, is the most necessary point of present wisdom: an important imagination, and the way to happiness.

THOMAS TRAHERNE

Day 228

The Highest Service

The highest service may be prepared for and done in the humblest surroundings. In silence, in waiting, in obscure, unnoticed offices, in years of uneventful unrecorded duties, the Son of God grew and waxed strong.

LELAND STANFORD

One Real Friend

True friendship multiplies the good in life and divides its evils. Strive to have friends, for life without friends is like life on a desert island. . .to find one real friend in a lifetime is good fortune; to keep him is a blessing.

BALTASAR GRACIAN

Day 230

Matters of Universal Interest

We do not need to be shoemakers to know if our shoes fit, and just as little have we any need to be professionals to acquire knowledge of matters of universal interest.

GEORG WILHELM FRIEDRICH HEGEL

Acquainted with History

A man acquainted with history may, in some respect, be said to have lived from the beginning of the world, and to have been making continual additions to his stock of knowledge in every century.

DAVID HUME

DAY 232

The Results of Faith

It is only by risking our persons from one hour to another that we live at all. And often enough our faith beforehand in an uncertified result is the only thing that makes the result come true.

WILLIAM JAMES

With One Mind

Nothing can be more absurd than the practice that prevails in our country of men and women not following the same pursuits with all their strengths and with one mind, for thus, the state instead of being whole is reduced to half.

PLATO

DAY 234

Designated for This Work

Many believe and I believe that I have been designated for this work by God. In spite of my old age, I do not want to give it up; I work out of love for God and I put all my hope in Him.

MICHELANGELO

As You Will

Every day that is born into the world comes like a burst of music and rings the whole day through, and you make of it a dance, a dirge, or a life march, as you will.

THOMAS CARLYLE

DAY 236

The Source of Strength and Grace

Never think that you can live to God by your own power or strength; but always look to and rely on him for assistance, yea, for all strength and grace.

DAVID BRAINERD

Heavenly Support

After I had given up to go, the thoughts of the journey were often attended with unusual sadness, in which times, my heart was frequently turned to the Lord with inward breathings for his heavenly support, that I might not fail to follow him wheresoever he might lead me.

JOHN WOOLMAN

A Hundred Virtues

Being forced to work, and forced to do your best, will breed in you temperance and self-control, diligence and strength of will, cheerfulness and content and a hundred virtues which the idle man will never know.

CHARLES KINGSLEY

The Absence of Gratitude

A person however learned and qualified in his life's work in whom gratitude is absent, is devoid of that beauty of character which makes personality fragrant.

HAZRAT INAYAT KHAN

Day 240

Soft Words and Hard Arguments

It is an excellent rule to be observed in all disputes, that men should give soft words and hard arguments; that they should not so much strive to vex as to convince each other.

JOHN WILKINS

Our Real Character

We learn our virtues from our friends who love us; our faults from the enemy who hates us. We cannot easily discover our real character from a friend. He is a mirror, on which the warmth of our breath impedes the clearness of the reflection.

JEAN PAUL

Day 242

An Overcomer's Mind

The boy who is going to make a great man. . . must make up his mind not merely to overcome a thousand obstacles, but to win in spite of a thousand repulses or defeats.

TEDDY ROOSEVELT

Don't Look Back

As soon as they had brought them out, one of them said, "Flee for your lives! Don't look back, and don't stop anywhere in the plain! Flee to the mountains or you will be swept away!" But Lot's wife looked back, and she became a pillar of salt.

GENESIS 19:17, 26 NIV

DAY 244

A Rule of Life

Make it a rule of life never to regret and never to look back. Regret is an appalling waste of energy; you can't build on it; it's only good for wallowing in.

KATHERINE MANSFIELD

The Right Moment

The right moment wears a full head of hair: when it has been missed, you can't get it back; it's bald in the back of the head and never turns around.

FRANÇOIS RABELAIS

Day 246

Shining Lights

It is very remarkable, that in the book of life,
we find some almost of all kinds of occupations,
who notwithstanding served God in their respective
generations, and shone as so many lights in the world.

GEORGE WHITEFIELD

Your Guide

Never think that Jesus has hidden away the riches of wisdom and knowledge, as in a treasure chest without a key or of your way as a path without a light. Jesus, who is your wisdom, is guiding you, even when you can't see it.

ANDREW MURRAY

Day 248

Be Swift to Love

Life is short and we have never too much time for gladdening the hearts of those who are travelling the dark journey with us. Oh be swift to love, make haste to be kind.

HENRI FREDERIC AMIEL

Only Sure of Today

Don't look back on happiness, or dream of it in the future. You are only sure of today; do not let yourself be cheated out of it.

HENRY WARD BEECHER

DAY 250

Every Concrete Opportunity

No matter how full a reservoir of maxims one may possess, and no matter how good one's sentiments may be, if one has not taken advantage of every concrete opportunity to act, one's character may remain entirely unaffected for the better.

WILLIAM JAMES

Mighty Faith

Faith, mighty faith the promise sees,
And looks to that alone;
Laughs at impossibilities,
And cries, "It shall be done!"

CHARLES WESLEY

Do It!

You must make sure of what you want to do; you must feel sure that you have the courage as well as the temperament to do it and then—do it!

HERBERT KAUFMAN

Digging Deep

Do you wish to be great? Then begin by being. Do you desire to construct a vast and lofty fabric? Think first about the foundations of humility. The higher your structure is to be, the deeper must be its foundation.

SAINT AUGUSTINE

DAY 254

No Failure

In God's world, for those who are in earnest, there is no failure. No work truly done, no word earnestly spoken, no sacrifice freely made, was ever made in vain.

FREDERICK WILLIAM ROBERTSON

Possessors of Wealth

The lust of avarice has so totally seized upon mankind that their wealth seems rather to possess them than they possess their wealth.

PLINY THE ELDER

Inner Peace

Never be in a hurry: do everything quietly and in a calm spirit. Do not lose your inward peace for anything whatsoever, even if your whole world seems upset.

FRANCIS DE SALES

Courage, Patience, Sleep

Have courage for the great sorrows of life and patience for the small ones; and when you have laboriously accomplished your daily task, go to sleep in peace. God is awake

VICTOR HUGO

DAY 258

Time Is Eternity

Time is too slow for those who wait, too swift for those who fear, too long for those who grieve, too short for those who rejoice, but for those who love, time is eternity.

HENRY VAN DYKE

Believe, Only Believe

Have your fondest schemes been blown upon, your fairest blossoms been withered in the bud? Has wave after wave been rolling upon you? Has the Lord forgotten to be gracious? Listen, hear the word of Jesus saying, "Believe, only believe." There is an infinite reason for the trial—a lurking thorn that requires removal; a gracious lesson that requires teaching.

E. M. BOUNDS

Day 260

Cultivate This Belief

Believe that with your feelings and your work you are taking part in the greatest; the more strongly you cultivate this belief, the more will reality and the world go forth from it.

RAINER MARIA RILKE

Well Done!

There is work for you to do; and by and by the harvest shall be gathered, and what a scene will be on the shore when we hear the Master on the throne shout, "Well done! Well done!" May the blessing of God fall upon us this afternoon, and let every man and woman be up and doing.

D. L. MOODY

DAY 262

Standing Close

Man goes far away or near but God never goes far-off; he is always standing close at hand, and even if he cannot stay within he goes no further than the door.

MEISTER ECKHART

At the Door

" 'Behold, I stand at the door and knock; if anyone hears My voice and opens the door, I will come in to him and will dine with him, and he with Me. He who has an ear, let him hear.' "

REVELATION 3:20, 22 NASB

Day 264

A Sovereign Antidote

A believing confidence in God is a sovereign antidote against prevailing despondency and a disquieted spirit. . . . When the soul embraces itself, it sinks; if it catches hold on the power and promise of God, it keeps the head above the billows.

MATTHEW HENRY

Knowledge of the Self

Knowledge of the self is the mother of all knowledge. So it is incumbent on me to know my self, to know it completely, to know its minutiae, its characteristics, its subtleties, and its very atoms.

KAHLIL GIBRAN

Life Hid with Christ

In order to enter into this blessed interior life of rest and triumph, you have two steps to take: first, entire abandonment; and second, absolute faith. . . .These two steps, definitely taken and unwaveringly persevered in, will certainly bring you out sooner or later into the green pastures and still waters of this higher Christian life.

HANNAH WHITALL SMITH

To Be Greatly Good

A man, to be greatly good, must imagine intensely and comprehensively; he must put himself in the place of another and of many others; the pains and pleasures of his species must become his own.

PERCY BYSSHE SHELLEY

The Intelligent Merchant

No man ever got very high by pulling other people down. The intelligent merchant does not knock his competitors. The sensible worker does not work those who work with him. Don't knock your friends. Don't knock your enemies. Don't knock yourself.

ALFRED LORD TENNYSON

Of What Stuff We Are Made

We must accept life for what it actually is—
a challenge to our quality without which we
should never know of what stuff we are made,
or grow to our full stature.

ROBERT LOUIS STEVENSON

The Measure of Success

I have learned that success is to be measured not so much by the position that one has reached in life as by the obstacles which he has overcome while trying to succeed.

BOOKER T. WASHINGTON

With Tranquility

In your occupations, try to possess your soul in peace. It is not a good plan to be in haste to perform any action that it may be the sooner over.
On the contrary, you should accustom yourself to do whatever you have to do with tranquillity, in order that you may retain the possession of yourself and of settled peace.

MADAME JEANNE GUYON

DAY 272

What Will Your Day Bring?

Whether any particular day shall bring to you more of happiness or of suffering is largely beyond your power to determine. Whether each day of your life shall give happiness or suffering rests with yourself.

GEORGE S. MERRIAM

The Divine Action

The divine action is ever fresh, it never retraces its steps, but always marks out new ways. Souls that are conducted by it never know where they are going; their ways are neither to be found in books, nor in their own minds; the divine action carries them step by step, and they progress only according to its movement.

JEAN PIERRE DE CAUSSADE

The Impossible Dream

To dream the impossible dream,
To fight the unbeatable foe,
To bear with unbearable sorrow
To run where the brave dare not go;
To right the unrightable wrong.
To love, pure and chaste, from afar,
To try, when your arms are too weary,
To reach the unreachable star!

JOE DARION

A Plan Working in Our Lives

There is a plan working in our lives; and if we keep our hearts quiet and our eyes open, it all works together; and if we don't, it all fights together, and goes on fighting till it comes right, somehow, somewhere.

ANNIE KEARY

Day 276

God's Will for Thee Now

Bear in the presence of God to know thyself. Then seek to know for what God sent thee into the world; how thou hast fulfilled it; art thou yet what God willed thee to be; what yet lacketh unto thee; what is God's will for thee now. . .what one thing thou mayest now do, by His grace, to obtain His favor, and approve thyself unto Him.

EDWARD B. PUSEY

Strength at the Moment Needed

Should we feel at times disheartened and discouraged, a confiding thought, a simple movement of heart towards God will renew our powers. Whatever He may demand of us, He will give us at the moment the strength and the courage that we need.

FRANÇOIS FÉNELON

Day 278

The Power of Composure

The mind never puts forth greater power over itself than when, in great trials, it yields up calmly its desires, affections, interests to God. There are seasons when to be still demands immeasurably higher strength than to act. Composure is often the highest result of power.

WILLIAM ELLERY CHANNING

Direct Religion

There are geniuses who, in the fathomless depths of abstraction and pure speculation. . .present their ideas to God. Their prayer audaciously offers an argument. Their worship questions. This is direct religion, filled with anxiety and responsibility for those who would scale its walls.

VICTOR HUGO

Bound to Be True

I am not bound to win, but I am bound to be true. I am not bound to succeed, but I am bound to live by the light that I have. I must stand with anybody that stands right, and stand with him while he is right, and part with him when he goes wrong.

ABRAHAM LINCOLN

Always Doing

Determine never to be idle. No person will have occasion to complain of the want of time who never loses any. It is wonderful how much may be done if we are always doing.

THOMAS JEFFERSON

DAY 282

Spiritual Sowing

Do not be deceived: God cannot be mocked. A man reaps what he sows. The one who sows to please his sinful nature, from that nature will reap destruction; the one who sows to please the Spirit, from the Spirit will reap eternal life.

GALATIANS 6:7–8 NIV

In the Field of Destiny

The tissue of the Life to be
We weave with colors all our own,
And in the field of Destiny
We reap as we have sown.

JOHN GREENLEAF WHITTIER

Day 284

A Hero's Vision

The prudent see only the difficulties, the bold only the advantages, of a great enterprise; the hero sees both; diminishes the former and makes the latter preponderate, and so conquers.

JOHANN KASPAR LAVATER

No Shrinking Back

There will be no misgiving, no shrinking back, no calculation of overpowering odds, no terror of possible consequences, if you frankly accept the gift which God offers you tomorrow.

JOSEPH B. LIGHTFOOT

Day 286

Unceasing Gifts

Often when He comes, He finds the soul occupied. Other guests are there, and He has to turn away. He cannot gain entry, for we love and desire other things; therefore, His gifts, which He is offering to everyone unceasingly, must remain outside.

JOHANNES TAULER

Our Impact

Nothing could be more simple, more intelligible, more natural, more supernatural. It is an analogy from an everyday fact. Since we are what we are by the impacts of those who surround us, those who surround themselves with the highest will be those who change into the highest.

HENRY DRUMMOND

Day 288

Trifling Things

Regard not the appearance of things you are to do, but Him who commands them, and who, when He pleases, can accomplish His glory and our perfection through the most trifling things. When a person thinks a duty is beneath him, he places himself above God, for He deals with that same duty.

LELAND STANFORD

Thank God for His Mercy

I have often met with happiness after some imprudent step which ought to have brought ruin upon me, and although passing a vote of censure upon myself I would thank God for his mercy.

GIACOMO CASANOVA

The Tamed Tongue

This is a truth that all of us who seek to influence our fellow beings. . .must lay to heart. The soft tongue breaketh the bone. The tamed tongue subdues the adversary.

WASHINGTON GLADDEN

A Challenge to Life

The most glorious moments in your life are not the so-called days of success, but rather those days when out of dejection and despair you feel rise in you a challenge to life, and the promise of future accomplishments.

GUSTAVE FLAUBERT

Something to Be Enthusiastic About

We act as though comfort and luxury were the chief requirements of life, when all that we need to make us really happy is something to be enthusiastic about.

CHARLES KINGSLEY

Character Is Credit

Nature has written a letter of credit upon some men's faces which is honored wherever presented. You cannot help trusting such men. Their very presence gives confidence. There is a "promise to pay" in their faces which gives confidence, and you prefer it to another man's endorsement. Character is credit.

WILLIAM MAKEPEACE THACKERAY

Day 294

Lofty Dreams

Dream lofty dreams, and as you dream, so you shall become. Your vision is the promise of what you shall one day be; your ideal is the prophecy of what you shall at last unveil.

JAMES ALLEN

The Great Theater of Life

No more duty can be urged upon those who are entering the great theater of life than simple loyalty to their best convictions.

EDWIN HUBBEL CHAPIN

Day 296

Love Made Visible

Work is love made visible. And if you cannot work with love but only with distaste, it is better that you should leave your work and sit at the gate of the temple and take alms of those who work with joy.

KAHLIL GIBRAN

Full Hope

Do not look forward to the changes and chances of this life in fear; rather look to them with full hope that, as they arise, God, whose you are, will deliver you out of them. He has kept you hitherto—do you but hold fast to His dear hand, and He will lead you safely through all things; and, when you cannot stand, He will bear you in His arms.

FRANCIS DE SALES

DAY 298

Three Teachers

Three men are my friends—he that loves me, he that hates me, he that is indifferent to me. He who loves me teaches me tenderness; he who hates me teaches me caution; he who is indifferent to me teaches me self-reliance. So long as we love, we serve. So long as we are loved by others, I would almost say we are indispensable.

THOMAS À KEMPIS

The Tests of Life

The tests of life are to make, not break us. . . . The blow at the outward man may be the greatest blessing to the inner man. If God, then, puts or permits anything hard in our lives, be sure that the real peril, the real trouble, is what we shall lose if we flinch or rebel.

MALTBIE D. BABCOCK

Day 300

The Book of Life

For the individual, the Bible—the Book of Life—teaches the art of individual growth, and it is a guide to conduct and character. . . . For the young man and woman, it is the rule for godly attitudes and behavior; for the tempted, it shows how to live victoriously. For everyone, the Bible is a roadmap for salvation.

NEWELL DWIGHT HILLIS

The Brave Man's Dictionary

Know that "impossible". . .has no place in the brave man's dictionary. That when all men have said "Impossible," and tumbled noisily elsewhither, and thou alone art left, then first thy time and possibility have come. It is for thee now; do thou that, and ask no man's counsel, but thy own only and God's.

THOMAS CARLYLE

Faith in Things Unseen

All the strength and force of man comes from his faith in things unseen. He who believes is strong, he who doubts is weak. Strong convictions precede great actions.

JAMES FREEMAN CLARKE

Mountain-Moving Faith

When you believe with all your heart, soul, and mind, you will move mountains. "Because of your faith, it will happen" (Matthew 9:29 NLT). "Nothing would be impossible" (Matthew 17:20 NLT). "Anything is possible if a person believes" (Mark 9:23 NLT).

Day 304

Positive Results

Success or failure depends more upon attitude than upon capacity. Successful men act as though they have accomplished or are enjoying something. Soon it becomes a reality. Act, look, feel successful, conduct yourself accordingly, and you will be amazed at the positive results.

WILLIAM JAMES

Asking Anything

Asking anything, getting everything, willing with God, praying with God, praising with God. . . . How can God trust us with a power so deep and terrible? Ah, He can trust the ideal life with anything. "If he ask anything." Well, if he does, he will ask nothing amiss. It will be God's will if it is asked. It will be God's will if it is not asked.

HENRY DRUMMOND

DAY 306

Fear Not

Weary and faint one! You have an Omnipotent arm to lean on. "He faints not, neither is weary!" Listen to His own gracious assurance: "Fear not, for I am with you. Do not be dismayed, for I am your God. I will strengthen you. . . ." Leaving all your false props and refuges, let this be your resolve—"I trust in the Lord for protection!"

JOHN MACDUFF

Walking in the Light

You have a disagreeable duty to do at twelve o'clock. Do not blacken nine and ten and eleven, and all between, with the color of twelve. Do the work of each, and reap your reward in peace. So when the dreaded moment in the future becomes the present, you shall meet it walking in the light, and that light will overcome its darkness.

GEORGE MACDONALD

DAY 308

An Endless Chain

Life stretches on like an endless chain, whose initial links we know not, nor yet those to come. But that we are each day the sum of all that we ever have been is a truth as undeniable as any of exact mathematics. We cannot skip a single link. One act, one mood, predetermines another.

LILIAN WHITING

Our Wealth

Our wealth is either advantageous or pernicious to us, according as we stand affected to it. If we make it our rest and our ruler, it will be our ruin; if we make it our servant, and an instrument of righteousness, it will be a blessing.

MATTHEW HENRY

Day 310

Exercising Patience

Hope has a thick skin, and will endure many a blow; it will put on patience as a vestment, it will wade through a sea of blood, it will endure all things, if it be of the right kind, for the joy that is set before it. . .it is hope that makes the soul exercise patience.

JOHN BUNYAN

Write Your Name

Live for something. Do good, and leave behind you a monument of virtue that the storm of time can never destroy. Write your name, in kindness, love, and mercy, on the hearts of thousands you come in contact with year by year; you will never be forgotten.

THOMAS CHALMERS

Day 312

Breaths of Prayer

A breath of prayer in the morning, and the morning life is sure. A breath of prayer in the evening, and the evening blessing comes. . . . Breath by breath our life comes into us. Inch by inch it is redeemed. So much prayer today—so many inches redeemed today.

HENRY DRUMMOND

Prefect Peace

"Thou wilt keep him in perfect peace whose mind is stayed on Thee: because he trusteth in Thee." This is. . .no speculative theory, neither is it a dream of romance. There *is* such a thing as having one's soul kept in perfect peace, now and here in this life; and childlike trust in God is the key to its attainment.

HANNAH WHITALL SMITH

Day 314

Maintain Your Position

If you maintain your position and say: "Lord, I am going to expect Thee to do Thy utmost, and I am going to trust Thee day by day to keep me absolutely," your faith will grow stronger and stronger, and you will know the keeping power of God in unbrokenness.

ANDREW MURRAY

God's Great Natural Law

If you would keep young and happy, cultivate hope, live a high moral life, practice the principles of the brotherhood of man, send out good thoughts and prayers to all, and think evil of no man. . . . This is in obedience to God's great natural law.

THOMAS BROOKS

Day 316

A Fixed Heart

A joyous man, such as I have now in my mind's eye, is for all intents and purposes a strong man. He is strong in a calm, restful manner. Whatever happens he is not ruffled or disturbed. He is not afraid of evil tidings; his heart is fixed, trusting in the Lord.

CHARLES SPURGEON

The Nature of God

Everyone who understands the nature of God rightly necessarily knows that God is to be believed and hoped in, that he is to be loved and called upon, and to be heard in all things.

WILLIAM AMES

Day 318

An Inward Spring

Imitation is mechanical, reflection organic. The one is occasional, the other habitual. In the one case, man comes to God and imitates Him; in the other, God comes to man and imprints Himself upon him . . . . Every character has an inward spring, let Christ be it. Every action has a key-note, let Christ set it.

HENRY DRUMMOND

But a Beginning

Before you learn to walk you have to crawl on all fours; to try to fly right before walking is a dangerous set-up. Certainly there must be great decisions, but even in connection with them the important thing is to get under way with *your* decision. Do not fly so high with your decisions that you forget that a decision is but a beginning.

SOREN KIERKEGAARD

DAY 320

Decision, Decisions

In any moment of decision, the best thing you can do is the right thing, the next best thing is the wrong thing, and the worst thing you can do is nothing.

TEDDY ROOSEVELT

One Refuge and Resource

However perplexed you may at any hour become about some question of truth, one refuge and resource is always at hand: you can do something for someone besides yourself. . . . Let this thought, then, stay with you: there may be times when you cannot find help, but there is no time when you cannot give help.

GEORGE S. MERRIAM

DAY 322

Sail Away from the Safe Harbor

Twenty years from now you will be more disappointed by the things that you didn't do than by the ones you did do. So throw off the bowlines. Sail away from the safe harbor. Catch the trade winds in your sails. Explore. Dream. Discover.

MARK TWAIN

Be Strong and Courageous!

"Be strong and courageous, and act; do not fear nor be dismayed, for the LORD God, my God, is with you. He will not fail you nor forsake you until all the work for the service of the house of the LORD is finished."

1 CHRONICLES 28:20 NASB

Day 324

Without Flinching

One ought never to turn one's back on a threatened danger and try to run away from it. If you do that, you will double the danger. But if you meet it promptly and without flinching, you will reduce the danger by half. Never run away from anything. Never!

WINSTON CHURCHILL

Step-by-Step

The true picture of life as it is, if it could be adequately painted, would show men what they are, and how they might rise, not, indeed, to perfection, but one step first, and then another on the ladder.

ANTHONY TROLLOPE

Good Speed

Think not any business or haste, though never so great, a sufficient excuse to omit prayer in the morning: But meditate—That the greater thy business is, by so much the more need thou hast to pray for God's good speed and blessing upon it, seeing it is certain that nothing can prosper without his blessing.

LEWIS BAYLY

The Still, Small Voice

So long as there is some thought of personal advantage, some idea of acquiring the praise and commendation of men, some aim at self-aggrandisement, it will be simply impossible to find out God's purpose concerning us. The door must be resolutely shut against all these if we would hear the still, small voice.

F. B. MEYER

Day 328

Be Wholly Still and Alone

It is not necessary that you leave the house. Remain at your table and listen. Do not even listen, only wait. Do not even wait, be wholly still and alone. The world will present itself to you for its unmasking, it can do no other, in ecstasy it will writhe at your feet.

FRANZ KAFKA

Encountering Everyday Epiphanies

Gratitude bestows reverence, allowing us to encounter everyday epiphanies, those transcendent moments of awe that change forever how we experience life and the world.

JOHN MILTON

DAY 330

Happy in the Interim

Change is certain. Peace is followed by disturbances; departure of evil men by their return. Such recurrences should not constitute occasions for sadness but realities for awareness, so that one may be happy in the interim.

PERCY BYSSHE SHELLEY

Life and Work

Life and work: beware of separating them. The more work you have, the more your work appears a failure. The more unfit you feel for work, take all the more time and care to have your inner life renewed in close fellowship with God.

ANDREW MURRAY

The Very Best Shape

All will be well in time. . . . What never ran smooth yet, can hardly be expected to change its character for us; so we must take it as we find it, and fashion it into the very best shape we can, by patience and good humor.

CHARLES DICKENS

A Change in Attitude

Could we change our attitude, we should not only see life differently, but life itself would come to be different. Life would undergo a change of appearance because we ourselves had undergone a change in attitude.

KATHERINE MANSFIELD

Day 334

A Safe Guide

The Bible, as a revelation from God, was not designed to give us all the information we might desire, nor to solve all the questions about which the human soul is perplexed, but to impart enough to be a safe guide to the haven of eternal rest.

ALBERT BARNES

Beginning Afresh

Be patient with everyone, but above all with yourself. I mean, do not be disturbed because of your imperfections, and always rise up bravely from a fall. I am glad that you make a daily new beginning; there is no better means of progress in the spiritual life than to be continually beginning afresh, and never to think that we have done enough.

FRANCIS DE SALES

DAY 336

Daily Strength

Think not that the strength of man shall ever be able to overcome the power of God. . . . The same God who directs the earth in its orbit, who feeds the burning furnace of the sun, and trims the lamps of heaven, has promised to supply you with daily strength.

CHARLES SPURGEON

Their Only Capital

A library book lasts as long as a house, for hundreds of years. It is not, then, an article of mere consumption but fairly of capital, and often in the case of professional men, setting out in life, it is their only capital . . . . I cannot live without books.

THOMAS JEFFERSON

Ask Boldly

I am prejudiced in favor of him who,
without impudence, can ask boldly. He has faith in humanity, and faith in himself. No one who is not accustomed to giving grandly can ask nobly and with boldness.

JOHANN KASPAR LAVATER

True Love

Love consists in giving without getting in return; in giving what is not owed, what is not due the other. That's why true love is never based, as associations for utility or pleasure are, on a fair exchange.

MORTIMER ADLER

Day 340

The Measure of Your Maturity

Maturity is the ability to think, speak and act your feelings within the bounds of dignity. The measure of your maturity is how spiritual you become during the midst of your frustrations.

SAMUEL ULLMAN

The Word *Finis*

Each of our passions, even love, has a stomach that must not be overloaded. We must in everything write the word *finis* in time; we must restrain ourselves, when it becomes urgent; we must draw the bolt on the appetite. . . . The wise man is he who knows when and how to stop.

VICTOR HUGO

DAY 342

Thinking Determines Life

Why should we think upon things that are lovely? Because thinking determines life. It is a common habit to blame life upon the environment. Environment modifies life but does not govern life. The soul is stronger than its surroundings.

WILLIAM JAMES

March Out Boldly

"You won't have to lift a hand in this battle; just stand firm. . .and watch GOD's saving work for you take shape. Don't be afraid, don't waver. March out boldly tomorrow—GOD is with you."

2 CHRONICLES 20:17 MSG

DAY 344

Begin It

What you can do, or dream you can, begin it.
Boldness has genius, power, and magic in it.
Only engage, and then the mind grows heated;
Begin it and the work will be completed.

JOHANN WOLFGANG VON GOETHE

Castles in the Air

If you have built castles in the air, your work need not be lost; that is where they should be. Now put the foundations under them.

HENRY DAVID THOREAU

DAY 346

Watered Gardens

Those who go forth ministering to the wants and necessities of their fellow beings experience a rich return, their souls being as a watered garden and as a spring that faileth not.

LUCRETIA MOTT

Our Divine Purpose

The choice that you, as a Soul, have in relation to anything is always to be loving. Do you understand that this is the divine purpose that all of us as humans have been given—to love unconditionally?

JOHN MORTON

Unexpected Places and Joys

The soul which follows in the footsteps of the Christ, and in poverty and hard work and misfortune bravely meets and nobly endures, will find light in unexpected places and joys where only fears were looked for.

GEORGE H. HEPWORTH

Ever After Dreams

I have dreamed in my life, dreams that have stayed with me ever after, and changed my ideas; they have gone through and through me, like wine through water, and altered the color of my mind.

EMILY BRONTË

Day 350

Working Wonders

It is not so true that "prayer changes things" as that prayer changes me and I change things. God has so constituted things that prayer on the basis of Redemption alters the way in which a man looks at things. Prayer is not a question of altering things externally, but of working wonders in a man's disposition.

OSWALD CHAMBERS

Light Enough to Steer By

There are things of which we may be positively certain though we cannot comprehend all their connections and relations. . . . Beyond our ken lie the mysteries unexplored. But we have light enough to steer by. We know as much as we need. If we live with hope, by it we shall know more someday.

JAMES MCCOSH

Day 352

Your Real Desire

If your real desire is to be good, there is no need to wait for the money before you do it; you can do it now, this very moment, and just where you are.

JAMES ALLEN

No Prompter Relief

Ask those who love Him with a sincere love, and they will tell you that they find no greater or prompter relief amid the troubles of their life than in loving conversation with their Divine Friend.

ALPHONSUS LIGUORI

DAY 354

Peace for the Journey

May the peace which no earthly disturbance can mar, which is of the Father through His inspiration and love, fill your hearts, and enable you to go on in the journey of life with a feeling of trust and confidence that nothing can disturb.

LELAND STANFORD

The Unimportant

Where I was born and where and how I have lived is unimportant. It is what I have done with where I have been that should be of interest.

DWIGHT L. MOODY

Any Good Thing

I expect to pass through this world but once; any good thing therefore that I can do, or any kindness that I can show to any fellow creature, let me do it now; let me not defer or neglect it, for I shall not pass this way again.

STEPHEN GRELLET

The Attitude You Bring

Your living is determined not so much by what life brings to you as by the attitude you bring to life; not so much by what happens to you as by the way your mind looks at what happens.

KAHLIL GIBRAN

Help Will Come

There is never a time when we may not hope in God. Whatever our necessities, however great our difficulties, and though to all appearance help is impossible, yet our business is to hope in God, and it will be found that it is not in vain. In the Lord's own time help will come.

GEORGE MÜLLER

All That Befalls

All that befalls you, to the very numbering of your hairs, is known to God! Nothing can happen by accident or chance. . . . The fall of the forest leaf—the fluttering of the insect—the waving of the angel's wing—the annihilation of a world—all are equally noted by Him. Man speaks of great things and small things—God knows no such distinction.

JOHN MACDUFF

DAY 360

How You Should Live

Do not let your faults discourage you. Be patient with yourself as well as with your neighbor. Thinking too much will exhaust you and cause you to make a lot of mistakes. Learn to pray in all your daily situations. Speak, act, and walk as if you were in prayer. This is how you should live anyway.

FRANÇOIS FÉNELON

A Good Haven

To desire and strive to be of some service to the world, to aim at doing something which shall really increase the happiness and welfare and virtue of mankind—this is a choice which is possible for all of us; and surely it is a good haven to sail for.

HENRY VAN DYKE

Day 362

The Road to Contentment

I do not think that the road to contentment lies in despising what we have not got. Let us acknowledge all good, all delight that the world holds, and be content without it.

GEORGE MACDONALD

Contentment and Confidence

Make sure that your character is free from the love of money, being content with what you have; for He Himself has said, "I WILL NEVER DESERT YOU, NOR WILL I EVER FORSAKE YOU," so that we confidently say, "THE LORD IS MY HELPER, I WILL NOT BE AFRAID. WHAT WILL MAN DO TO ME?"

HEBREWS 13:5–6 NASB

DAY 364

Watching for Opportunities

What helps luck is a habit of watching for opportunities, of having a patient but restless mind, of sacrificing one's ease or vanity, of uniting a love of detail to foresight, and of passing through hard times bravely.

C. VICTOR CHERBULIEZ

Go Forth without Fear

Look not mournfully into the Past. It comes not back again. Wisely improve the Present. It is thine. Go forth to meet the shadowy Future, without fear, and with a manly heart.

HENRY WADSWORTH LONGFELLOW

Notes: